The Comparison Trap

*Celebrating
how God
made you*

PRESENTED BY

Jill Briscoe

NexGen™ is an imprint of
Cook Communications Ministries, Colorado Springs, Colorado 80918
Cook Communications, Paris, Ontario
Kingsway Communications, Eastbourne, England

THE COMPARISON TRAP
© 2003 by *Just Between Us* magazine

First Printing, 2003
Printed in the United States of America

1 2 3 4 5 6 7 8 9 10 Printing/Year 07 06 05 04 03

This book is part of a series on relevant issues for today's Christian woman. For more information on other titles in this series or for information about *Just Between Us* magazine, please turn to the back of this book.

Library of Congress Cataloging-in-Publication Data
The comparison trap : celebrating how God made you / [edited by] Jill Briscoe.
    p. cm. -- (Just between us)
  ISBN 0-7814-3950-7 (booklet : pbk.)
  1. Christian women--Religious life. 2. Self-acceptance in
women--Religious aspects--Christianity. I. Briscoe, Jill. II. Series.
  BV4527.C635 2003
  248.8'43--dc21
                                        2003006661

A Note from Jill Briscoe

Dear Friends,

"Oh, Lord," I breathed as I sat on the platform at a meeting. "Look at that chic speaker three chairs down. Why did I wear beige? They won't be able to see me against the curtains!"

I've always struggled with comparisons. I had a sister I adored and I wanted to be just like her. I had a friend with cute freckles on her nose and I wanted freckles too. I played tournament tennis and I wanted to perfect my backhand and make it look like my Wimbledon idol.

It didn't help when I became a Christian either. In fact it grew worse. I looked around at the new friends I had made and found an inordinate desire to walk like them, talk like them, witness like them, pray like them, and know the Bible like them. It was a trap—a comparison trap—and this little church mouse was caught securely in it.

Half of the problem was my own insecurity. Another piece of my problem was a sincere desire to be the very best for God, and when I saw someone doing that, I tried to copy her. Comparisons usually lead to copying and that is not all bad if you copy the principles and not the particulars.

You can't copy spiritual gifts, however, even if you have gifts in the same area. God has made us uniquely and intends for each of us to be ourselves. Escaping the comparison trap is a question of being sure of your own identity.

The most freeing thought for me has been, "If I were them, who'd be me?" Why would God make me one of a kind if He wanted me to try being a clone?

Over the years, I've noted that the worst group for falling into the comparison trap is ministry wives who find themselves following a *perfect* predecessor. No matter what, just smile and insist on being you!

Hopefully those of you who battle with comparison will find the chapters in this book full of helpful hints and practical ways to escape it!

In His Love,

Jill Briscoe

chapter one

Conquering
Compassion

Victory begins by accepting who you are.
Meredith R. Sheppard

The woman I listened to on the phone tearfully related how inferior she felt to the other students in her Bible class, largely made up of fellow church members—young and old, professionals and plain old Joes, Ph.D.s and "GEDs." When the instructor asked questions or called for comments, if a "professional" responded, this precious woman clammed up, retreating to the inner recesses of her thickening shell. Week after week this was her practice. An unwilling captive of comparison, imprisoned by tormenting thoughts of inadequacy and failure, she wavered between finishing the course and quitting.

A teen girl, straight-A student, recipient of numerous awards and scholarships, who has the looks and poise of a model, struggles with feeling bad about herself and is often unaware of her abilities. While digging to find the root of her discontent she surprised me with a ready response, "I know why I feel this way... I'm comparing myself to others."

Sadly, I've had similar conversations with many

women, including ministry wives. One bright, articulate ministry wife felt "less than" because she is not college educated.

Being in the company of ministry wives who have college and/or seminary degrees caused her to regret having made a different educational and career choice many years ago. When consumed with comparing herself to others, she lost sight of her giftedness and God-given ability to minister effectively. However, when this ministry wife confronted comparison as sin and repented of how she let it control her life, a newfound freedom and self-acceptance was discovered.

When we struggle with comparison, we are usually comparing our weaknesses to the strengths of another. Consequently we mistakenly assume others think or feel about us the way we think or feel about ourselves.

God told Moses to send men to explore the land of Canaan, which He promised to give to the Israelites. Moses chose twelve leaders to explore Canaan and come back with a thorough report of the land, its produce, the people, and their villages. Although the men came back boasting of the land's bounty, they were fearful of its inhabitants. "The land we explored devours those living in it. All the people we saw there are of great size ... We seemed like grasshoppers in our own eyes, and we looked the same to them," (Num. 13:32-33).

By comparing themselves to the inhabitants of Canaan, the Israelites lost sight of who they were, whose they were, and God's promise to give them the land. Their fear led to faithlessness and disbelief, which caused God to become angry with them. "How long will this people treat me with contempt? How long will they refuse to believe in Me, in spite of all the miraculous signs I have performed among them?" (Num. 14:11).

By comparing ourselves to other women we too can lose sight of who we are, whose we are, and the promises and plans God gives us. Fear of not measuring up can lead to faithlessness and disbelief, born of discouragement. It also grieves the Holy Spirit.

Before you can ever find and enjoy fulfillment as a Christian woman, you must know who you are. There will always be the inner and outer voices telling you who you should be and what you should be doing. Resisting the temptation to listen to and heed those voices will keep you from the frustration of spinning off into a thousand different destructive directions.

Whenever someone shares with me their struggle with comparison, I share with them the following Scriptures: "We do not dare to classify or compare ourselves with some who commend themselves. When they measure themselves by themselves and compare themselves with themselves, they are not wise. ... But, 'Let him who boasts boast in the Lord.' For it is not the one who commends himself who is approved, but the one whom the Lord commends" (2 Cor. 10:12, 17-18).

"[Sisters] think of what you were when you were called. Not many of you were wise by human standards; not many were influential; not many were of noble birth. But God chose the foolish things of the world to shame the wise; God chose the weak things of the world to shame the strong. He chose the lowly things of this world and the despised things—and the things that are not—to nullify the things that are, so that no one may boast before him. It is because of him that you are in Christ Jesus, who has become for us wisdom from God—that is, our righteousness, holiness and redemption. Therefore, as it is written: 'Let him who boasts boast in the Lord'" (1 Cor. 1:26-31).

Remember the twelve explorers Moses chose to spy out Canaan? Two of the twelve, Joshua and Caleb, brought back a different report. Believing God's promise to give them the land, Caleb said, "We should go up and take possession of the land, for we can certainly do it ... The land we passed through and explored is exceedingly good. If the LORD is pleased with us, He will lead us into that land, a land flowing with milk and honey, and will give it to us. Only do not rebel against the LORD. And do not be afraid of the people of the land, because we will swallow them up. Their protection is gone, but the LORD is with us. Do not be afraid of them," (Num. 13:30; 14:7-9).

I challenge you to become like Joshua and Caleb who, despite their circumstances, believed God. If you believe God's Word and you act upon it, you too can conquer comparison.

chapter two

People Pleaser
or God-Pleaser—
Which One Are You?

Michele Halseide

I am a people-pleaser. I work overtime to please, impress, and placate friends and strangers because I need their affirmation to feel good about myself — especially my appearance.

I won't go to the grocery store without putting on makeup. I feel naked without blush and mascara. I imagine the checker whispering to the bagger, "Look at that woman! Her eyes are sinking into her head."

Unfortunately, my insecurities don't stop there. An unhealthy self-consciousness has somehow oozed into every area of my life, affecting how I spend my time and money, how I raise my children and set my priorities, even how I relate to other people.

I am not alone, however. Many women I meet are people-pleasers in one way or another. Take Jan, for instance. She over-prepares for routine meetings because she always wants to appear competent. Amanda won't invite a neighbor into her home unless it's spotless. And Debbie hosts extravagant birthday parties for her children — not so much to please them as to impress their guests' parents.

The Hidden Cost

We pay an enormous price for fretting over our approval rating.

"I catch myself telling little white lies," Sheila confesses. "Just the other day I told my cleaning lady we couldn't afford her anymore, when really I was firing her for doing a crummy job."

People-pleasers are easily conned into competing for worthless accolades—often running ourselves into the ground in the process. We judge ourselves by others' standards and reel with pain when we don't measure up. We pass up opportunities to talk about Jesus because we're too afraid to risk failure.

Simple joys are often sacrificed when we're preoccupied with what others think. "My weakest moment comes on Sunday morning when I have to fight with my kids to get them to wear itchy sweaters or loafers to church," says Mindy. "I know how they feel. But I think I worry more about our family's image than their comfort—or the sanctity of a peaceful Sunday morning."

People-pleasers often make choices that lead to sinful behaviors or poor stewardship of time and money. Teenagers can't say no to sex or drugs. Women rack up huge credit card bills enlarging their wardrobes beyond need or practicality. But worst of all, we may even be tempted to fake our spirituality, which impresses everyone but God.

"Be careful not to do your 'acts of righteousness' before men, to be seen by them," Christ warned.

"If you do, you will have no reward from your Father in heaven" (Matt. 6:1).

God is a jealous ruler who demands exclusive devotion to Himself (Exod. 34:14; Deut. 4:24; Josh. 24:19). We arouse His jealousy when we make idols out of ordinary people and derive our significance from the praises of men (Ps. 78:58). As we get sidetracked trying to win approval, we load our schedules with activities that appear worthwhile but actually keep us from the very things God prepared in advance for us to do (Eph. 2:10). I know a gifted writer, for example, who never gets to write because she's bogged down with the PTA, Girl Scouts, and several church committees. When I questioned her unwillingness to relinquish those responsibilities, she replied, "I couldn't drop the ball now. Everyone would hate me."

Do You Have Gumption?

There is a better way to live, and Mary, Martha's sister, found it (Luke 10:40-42). She wasn't worried about pleasing houseguests; she didn't need their approval. Mary had one overriding priority: to sit at Jesus' feet, stare into His eyes, and listen to God's Word.

David had the same passion. "One thing I ask of the LORD, this is what I seek: that I may dwell in the house of the LORD all the days of my life, to gaze upon the beauty of the LORD and to seek him in his temple," (Ps. 27:4).

Mary and David understood that we are transformed in the presence of the Lord. That is why our quest for significance and approval begins—and ends—with God. We will never grow in our relationship with God if we don't have the gumption to become single-minded, bent on pleasing God—and God only.

That sounds like a lofty, impractical goal in a world that measures success by how well we juggle demands for our attention. But such a change in orientation, though supernatural, *can* happen with the help of the Holy Spirit. Here are some practical measures that are helping me seek approval exclusively from God.

> ### LifeLifters
> "*G*reat opportunities to serve God rarely present themselves but little ones are frequent."
> —**Francis de Sales**—

Find out when *and* why *you feel insecure.* Whenever you catch yourself saying or doing something to impress others, make a mental note and later record your observations in a two-column journal. After filling in a few pages, you will begin to see a pattern. Try to determine its cause. Are you afraid of rejection or failure? Is pride the problem, low self-esteem, or even envy? Tracking these patterns also helps you anticipate situations that might cause you to feel anxious about your approval rating.

I noticed, for example, that in social settings such as a luncheon, I felt like a gawky teenager. To put myself on even ground with the other women, I usually resorted to boosting my self-image by name-dropping and talking about my husband's business or my writing projects.

Once I identified this behavior, I spent months

trying to understand it. I suspect that envy motivates me at times. I'd love to look good and appear in control of my life. But its deepest root comes from my childhood. My mom was always making fun of me and rarely took my interests seriously. As a child, I often felt embarrassed about who I was and what I liked to do.

Even today, I feel slightly out of place in a room full of adults, as if the clothes I'm wearing came out of a dress-up box. But understanding this insecurity helps me overcome it. Now when I go to luncheons, I avoid talking about myself and concentrate on asking other people questions. But most importantly, I have taken my fear of humiliation to the Lord, and He is rebuilding my confidence. Sometimes the Holy Spirit shows me a Scripture that strengthens my convictions about the inner beauty He is working to create within me. But God also has given me several "spiritual" moms who are helping me mature as an adult.

Plan alternative responses. In the column next to your list of people-pleasing slip-ups, jot down God-pleasing alternatives and specific Scriptures to support them. This will help you react more appropriately the next time you face similar circumstances.

Several years ago, for example, I accepted the treasurer's position at my children's preschool, fearing that if I turned down the job, other moms might accuse me of not doing my fair share. It ended up taking a lot of time away from my kids and my writing. Next to an entry in my journal where I wrote, "Succumbed to peer pressure again," I added, "I should have said, 'I have to pray about this. I'll let you know tomorrow.' Or, 'It's not fair to my family to assume such a heavy responsibility at this time.' Supportive Scripture: 'When a man's ways are pleasing to the LORD, he makes even his enemies live at peace with him'" (Prov. 16:7).

Change your thinking. Ask God to show you attitudes in need of change. I've found, for example, that I'm highly motivated by praise and easily discouraged by criticism. But tuning out certain criticisms requires discipline, a hard outer shell, and a soft inner heart for God. As I grow more deeply in love with Jesus, as I spend more time at His feet, it's easier to ignore nagging insecurities.

Stop judging others. We often expect people to judge us by the very same standards we are busy judging them by. If you make fun of another woman's taste in clothes, or the way she keeps house or manages her life, then you probably assume that other women are busy noting similar aspects about your lifestyle. In other words, a critical spirit feeds self-consciousness, and needlessly so. You'll start liking yourself more when you start judging others less.

We must learn to view people as God does. God told Samuel, "The LORD does not look at the things man looks at. Man looks at the outward appearance, but the LORD looks at the heart" (1 Sam. 16:7). Many wonderful surprises await us when we learn to fix our attention on the heart, not the hair.

Dwell upon the truth. Develop a list of Scriptures that lambaste the sources of your insecurities, and try to memorize them. When I'm feeling worthless and rejected, for instance, I recite my own condensed version of Isaiah 43:1-4: "Fear not, for I have redeemed you; I have summoned you by name; you are Mine ... You are precious and honored in My sight."

Your goal is to undergo a positive form of brainwashing. When you bathe your belief system in God's Word, it gradually changes you for the better. Together with praise and prayer, God's Word has divine power to demolish thoughts and insecurities that come from Satan (2 Cor. 10:4). But we must do our part; we must "take captive every thought to make it obedient to Christ" (v. 5). And that's what dwelling on the truth is all about.

Dare to change. When Mindy recognized that God was interested in her mindset for Sunday worship, not her outfit, she relaxed the family dress code. "At first I was embarrassed that my sons weren't the best-dressed kids in Sunday school," Mindy says. "But that feeling soon went away, especially when I began to see how it changed our family."

I admit I haven't completely conquered my fear of rejection, but it hasn't conquered me. Now when a neighbor knocks at my door—and I'm still in my bathrobe—I force myself to remember that when Jesus looks into my eyes, He sees the presence of God's Spirit. Not my eyelashes. And certainly not my pale complexion.

chapter three

Would
The Real Me
Please Stand Up?

Anita Haney

*L*ast week while cleaning out my closet,
I uncovered the dreaded envelope filled with
photographs that have been carefully hidden now for
almost eighteen years. They're photos I hate to look at,
yet I can't bring myself to destroy them. In a strange
sense, I need them—I need to refer to them from time
to time so I can remember, appreciate life and health,
and offer praise to God. I opened the envelope and
slowly fingered through each photo, one at a time,
smiling at some, which held memories of fun events,
of my family and friends, but each representing secret
pain and despair.

From February to June in 1982, I was hospitalized
with the eating disorder anorexia nervosa. Those four
months on a psychiatric ward marked the beginning
of my journey to find the real me—the person who
had somehow become lost amid a lifetime of
performing on many different "stages." Wearing one
mask for this person and then immediately switching

masks for the next person, changing myself to fit into so many different molds, had finally taken its toll on my life. The photos proved it.

It was hard for me to believe the person in those photos was really me. I viewed each phase of the disorder's progress as I flipped through the stack of memories. The telltale signs appeared— dark circles under my sunken eyes, my skeleton-thin torso, which shocked even me now. The photos mentally carried me back to an unreal seventy-six pounds. In the photos I was smiling, but I know now what was really hidden underneath that forced, faked exterior. Proverbs 14:13 says, "Even in laughter the heart may ache. ..."

Having been raised in a conservative pastor's home, and then growing up and falling in love with a preacher-boy, who later became a pastor himself, I had unknowingly lived life in a performance trap. As a child I not only wanted to make my parents proud and happy, but I also bent over backward to please every parishioner in each church where we ministered. That impossible goal continued into adulthood. I could not allow failure. I wanted to live up to the position I'd been placed in I wanted to succeed. Our family had to be perfect. Unfor-

> ### LifeLifters
>
> "*The* truth is nobody gets everything in life, not even those to whom you compare yourself. You have your good traits and your bad. The Bible's admonition is for us to accept without complaint both the good and bad we have been given. We are to work to make the most of what we have."
>
> —**Marlin Vis**—

tunately, the only person whose "perfection" I could control was my own, or so I thought. So I set out on a do-or-die mission to be all things to all people, even if it meant becoming a chameleon that switched colors to match her surroundings from minute to minute. As long as every single person was pleased with me, it didn't matter to me whether I was happy or not.

The downward spiral that years and years of fakery and pretense had brought on landed me, at age thirty, in a hospital due to my weakened physical condition, and then on to a psychiatric ward. I was separated from a loving husband who tried his best to understand; from my three precious children ages three, six, and eight at the time, who needed their mom and didn't understand; and from our church congregation who lovingly tried to help me through this bizarre time.

The four months of intensive treatment found me battling the depths of depression. Just the stigma and fears of realizing I was in a facility for mentally ill patients was a blow against hope or anything positive. Painful daily counseling sessions with a psychiatrist who specialized in eating disorders helped me to slowly peel back the many layers of masks that had been my security blanket, shields I had erected to guard my "perfection."

The day that hurt the most was when I finally had to look reality in the eye and come face-to-face with the fact that no matter how hard I worked I would never be able to be perfect. Even if I killed myself trying, I would never be all things to all people. That was the turning point for me. I finally knew I had to face up to the truth of "You can please all of the people some of the time and some of the people all of the time, but you can never please all of the people all of the time." I hated that! I didn't want it to be true!

But God, through His Word, softened my heart and began to break up the fallow soil so that truth could take root and grow and flourish. Paul hits the target in Galatians 1:10 with, "Am I now trying to win the approval of men, or of God? Or am I trying to please men? If I were still trying to please men, I would not be a servant of Christ." And also in 1 Corinthians 10:31, "So whether you eat or drink or whatever you do, do it all for the glory of God." Not the glory of men or women; not so you'll hear how awesome you are, how organized and efficient you are, or how happy and pleased you make every person and situation, but for the glory of God.

It has taken me forty-seven years to finally allow God to "form me into another pot, shaping me as seems best to Him" (see Jer. 18:1-6). I have had to endure the real pain of giving Him the liberty of smashing the clay (me) into a new ball in His hands in order to fashion and mold it into a new pot, one that's more fitted for His usefulness. In allowing that to happen, I've discovered that it's not that I've had to give up so much, but, instead, I have *received* so much. I'm just now comprehending a little of the *abundant living* He wants to give us and not just the *living.* When my focus shifted from myself and other people to God and what He wanted from me, everything else fell into its proper place.

I'm not saying that I never stumble by panicking over what someone thinks of me. I still do, but I'm not crushed nor driven by it any longer. I was told that anorexia nervosa is a lot like alcoholism. I'll always have the potential of being in bondage to it and of "falling off the wagon." But when I focus on the Word, the only truth, and the fact that my body is the temple of the Holy Spirit who is in me, and that I am not my own, but I was bought at a price, it is a great motivator to honor God (1 Cor. 6:19-20).

It's just like every other lesson we learn in living and in being like Christ; it's a daily, progressive journey. Sometimes you fall down, but you get up, brush yourself off, admit it to God, and learn how to do things differently the next time, so as to possess more of His traits and not your own.

The most powerful, liberating, peace-giving truth for me was learning that God created me just like I am and wants to use *me*, the *real me*, to do a work for Him.

"Such confidence as this is ours through Christ before God. Not that we are competent in ourselves to claim anything for ourselves, but our competence comes from God" (2 Cor. 3:4-5).

chapter four

Avoiding the Ministry Comparison Trap

Learning to appreciate
the resources God has given you.

Jill Briscoe

We need to be careful that our sense of value isn't determined by our resources, the numbers that turn up to worship, or the amount of the offerings given on the Lord's Day. It's hard to learn that lesson. Many of us feel we have been working hard at getting nowhere, that our wheels are spinning and, to make matters worse, everybody we meet who goes to another church tells us of innovative programs, special speakers, huge successful events, and a budget that has been met without mentioning money! It's discouraging when the church across the street is getting larger while we are getting smaller, and our slide projector keeps breaking down while the new fellowship on the block uses multi media on three screens every week. It's hard not to fall into the trap of "comparing" or simply giving up. "If only we had more money, overhead projectors, and wireless microphones," we lament. But the latest gadgets aren't everything.

While traveling in Africa and visiting missionaries, I noted with amusement a poster with the words,

We the unwilling
led by the unknowing
are doing the impossible
for the ungrateful.
We have done so much
for so long with so little,
we are now qualified
to do anything
with nothing!

I wonder if you can relate to that? Yet the greatest resource God has is people, and people have the Holy Spirit. Other priceless helps for us mortals are prayer, fellowship, the promises of God from the Word of God, and faith. Add all that to a person, and you have some pure spiritual resources to draw on that can empower you to do anything that needs doing. How do we know? Jesus said so. He said that with faith (not earth movers) we could move mountains. Paul said so, too. He even went so far as to say, "When I am weak then I am strong!" What's more, our "nothingness" gives God a chance to fill us with His "somethingness" and blow the devil away! Little is much when God is in it.

A great deal can be done for the kingdom by "little servants" with "little skill" and "little training" if they have big hearts for God. Proverbs 30:24-28 tells us about four small things God created that made up for their size by their wisdom. The ants have "little" strength, yet they use what they have to provide for their families. The coneys have "little" power, but they use the little they have to protect their homes. The locusts have no great leader, but they have fellowship with like-minded locusts and find that there is power in numbers. And the lizard is small enough to be held in the hand, but that gives it grand ideas of possessing the high ground. In other words, little is big if God is in it!

You, like me, may sometimes feel like an ant, coney, locust, or lizard, or any other small and rather ridiculous creature. But each of us has, like all of God's live created beings, capabilities far beyond our physical means or size. "If any of you lacks wisdom, he should ask God, who gives generously to all without finding fault, and it will be given to him" (James 1:5). God is God and I am me, but God and me together means that He is well able to work His wonders through me.

This is not to say that resources are not gifts, tools, and means to an end and should all be used, if available, to further kingdom work. I must confess, however, that I have found myself far more nervous when I have had to rely on complicated computers for sound and light presentations, fine-tuned microphones, and intricate and complicated production panels when presenting a musical drama to thousands of people (as has been my experience), than when in the past I have had to stand up in front of masses of wild street kids without any means of amplification at all. I well remember, while engaged in street evangelism, being searingly conscious of the need for God's provision, protection, and power. I had no help then but the power of the Spirit, the Word of

God, and the fellowship of a tiny "scared-to-death" team of helpers, whose saving faith was one great burning desire to reach for the stars and tell that mob about the One who made them. Sometimes I yearn for and miss the thrill of that latter experience while thoroughly enjoying and utilizing to the full the former.

Let's thank God for whatever "helps" that, in the economy of God, have been permitted to us, refuse to compare and allow a lack of material resources to frustrate us or dampen our spirits, and remember that "people" are God's most precious resources. So whether with a combine harvester or the "old-fashioned way" with rakes and pitchforks, lets bring in the harvest!

This excerpt from Renewal on the Run: Encouragement for Wives Who Are Partners in Ministry *is reprinted with permission from Harold Shaw Publishers, Box 587, Wheaton, IL 60189, copyright 1992.*

chapter five

Training
Your Soul
to Be Thankful

Shelly Esser

In the book, *Streams in the Desert*, Mrs. Charles Cowman tells the story "of a king who went into his garden one morning, and found everything withered and dying. He asked the oak that stood near the gate what the trouble was. He found it sick of life and determined to die because it was not tall and beautiful like the pine. The pine was all out of heart because it could not bear grapes, like the vine. The vine was going to throw its life away because it could not stand erect and have as fine fruit as the peach tree. The geranium was fretting because it was not tall and fragrant like the lilac; and so on all through the garden. Coming to a heart's-ease he found its bright face lifted and cheery as ever.

"'Well, heart's-ease, I'm glad amidst all this discouragement, to find one brave little flower. You do not seem to be the least disheartened.'

"'No, I am not of much account, but I thought that if you wanted an oak, or a pine, or a peach tree, or a lilac, you would have planted one; but as I knew you wanted a heart's-ease, I am determined to be the best little heart's-ease that I can.'"

I wonder how many of us can relate to this story. I know I can. Especially as women—like the trees and flowers in the garden—we find it so easy to compare ourselves to others. Before we know it, we fall into the trap of comparing our gifts, our ministries, and our churches with those around us, burying ourselves under the weight of always falling short. That kind of thinking has often left me frustrated, fretting like the poor little pine or peach tree because I'm trying to be someone I wasn't created to be or have a life I wasn't meant to have.

The little heart's-ease discovered one of the secrets for rooting out comparison. He stood out among the rest in the garden because he learned how to be content; he was happy with who he was and subsequently exhibited a willingness to be the best he could be in the place of his appointment.

Playing the comparison game forces us to look longingly at all we don't have instead of all we do have, resulting in a cancer of the perspective. It ultimately leads us into a preoccupation with ourselves. Before we realize it, self-centered attitudes such as "Am I good enough?" "Pretty enough?" "Gifted enough?" creep up on us, robbing us of all that's good in our life. It is here that the enemy snares us to keep us from appreciating all that God has given to us.

Another secret to defeating comparison is simply practicing thankfulness. If we're to overcome comparison, we need to train our souls to be thankful. Have you ever noticed how your outlook in life instantly changes when you choose to be thankful? Thankfulness enables us to focus on all we do have in *our* lives instead of on what *somebody else* has in her life. An ungrateful spirit is filled with things we aren't getting or don't have, whereas the thankful heart embraces what God has given to us and done for us. It's being able to look at how God is using *me* instead of focusing on why He's using *someone else* in a given capacity.

First Thessalonians 5:18 tells us, that we are to "give thanks in all circumstances, for this is God's will for you in Christ Jesus." This includes giving thanks for how God has made us. God has something wonderful in mind for each of us that no one else can do quite as well. So we need to put our false perceptions aside and ask ourselves, "What is the best way—given my gifts and abilities—to fulfill the calling God has given to *me*? When I focus on these things, my heart is freed from the feeling of needing to be like someone else. God didn't make us all alike, anyway. If we're not careful, looking at how others do it can eventually crush us, leading us to be more discontent and ungrateful. It can also prevent us from doing things the way God wants us to do them.

Paul very wisely said in 1 Cor. 12:4-6, that "there are different kinds of gifts ... service ... working." We shouldn't try to duplicate what others are doing. Realizing this truth has brought me tremendous freedom to be all I am in Christ—to be me! Being thankful gives us the ability to love life, to love others, and to love ourselves.

Author Luci Swindoll said, "The more we demand, grab for, complain about, worry over, the less we can value, cherish, savor, enjoy and accept. To look for the many little blessings is a choice we can all make." What good advice.

A couple of years ago my sister gave me a "gratitude journal." It has been an excellent tool in helping me to regularly reflect on all I have to be thankful for. Whenever I'm comparing myself to others and feeling sorry for myself, I start writing down all the things I have to be thankful for and almost instantaneously my perspective is transformed. A gratitude journal will change the way you see your life by helping to point your heart in the right direction, because the thing most often lacking in our lives is the awareness of how much we truly have.

> ### Life Lifters
>
> "*If* you are not satisfied with a little, you will not be satisfied with much."
>
> —**Edythe Draper**—

Next time you're tempted to compare yourself to someone else, remember that God wants to use you in the place of His calling, a place that only you can fill in His garden of life. Then you will be able to shine contentedly like the little heart's-ease, "No, I am not of much account, but I thought that if you wanted an oak, or a pine, or a peach tree, or a lilac, you would have planted one; but as I knew you wanted a heart's-ease, I am determined to be the best little heart's-ease that I can."

List 10 Things for Which You're Thankful

(Begin to make it a daily habit!)

"Praise the Lord, O my soul, and *forget not all his benefits* ..." (Psalm 103:2)

1.

2.

3.

4.

5.

6.

7.

8.

9.

10.

chapter six

How's Your *Resume?*

By refusing to play the comparison game, you can
fulfill your unique role in God's plan.

Cheryl M. Smith

*I*f God is the judge of success, what do we do
with the opinions of others? Do we listen to
their criticisms or praise, or do we simply write them
off?

Paul struggled with criticism. (So if you've been
criticized unfairly recently, take heart and consider
yourself in good company.) It seems that some of the
Corinthians felt Paul simply didn't match up with his
writings or with other speakers they had heard. How
did he handle their accusations? He handled them by
refusing to play the comparison game. Paul knew we
each have our own unique role in God's kingdom. If
we are going to boast, we should boast only in
fulfilling that which God has called us to do. As the
Bible says, "'Let him who boasts boast in the Lord.' For
it is not the one who commends himself who is
approved, but the one whom the Lord commends"
(2 Cor. 10:17-18).

The Comparison Game

This truth hit home in my life early in our first pastorate. True to my perfectionistic nature, I was very intent on meeting the church's expectations and fulfilling my role as the pastor's wife. This meant that I had a mental checklist against which I daily measured my performance. Included on my list of "things a good pastor's wife does" were:

- attends all church functions,
- sets the example in hospitality,
- visits church members with her husband,
- contributes her talents in music, teaching, and so on,
- assumes (gladly), and executes (competently) various leadership roles, such as women's functions, Sunday school, and so on,
- stays on top of things both spiritually and emotionally.

I'll conclude my list there. Amazingly, there were still many more qualifications I was trying to meet. I'm sure you get the idea. But no one can always meet everyone's expectations, and there was certainly no way I could live up to my own. As the mother of a toddler who was soon confronted with the arrival of another infant, my reality called for goals that had to do with simply making it through the day! To realize the expectations I had set for myself, I needed a clone—one to stay home and deal with the day-to-day, another to do all the work of the "ministry."

The result of this pressure was that my life was literally torn apart! Instead of maintaining emotional and spiritual control, I began a downward spiral into the dark abyss of clinical depression. And in my despair, I struggled with an overwhelming sense of failure, alienation, and tremendous anger toward God. After all, He had called me here to be a pastor's wife and now my entire world was falling apart!

It was about then I came across 1 Corinthians 4:3-5: "I care very little if I am judged by you or by any human court; indeed, I do not even judge myself. My conscience is clear, but that does not make me innocent. It is the Lord who judges me. Therefore judge nothing before the appointed time; wait till the Lord comes. He will bring to light what is hidden in darkness and will expose the motives of men's hearts. At that time each will receive his praise from God."

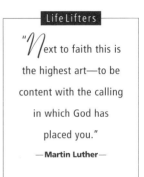

Life Lifters

"*Next* to faith this is the highest art—to be content with the calling in which God has placed you."

—**Martin Luther**—

I want you to notice several things from this passage. First, it is truly a small thing what other people think of us. We should be humble enough to consider their criticisms or praise. If there is merit in it, receive it. Yet, all in all, the opinions of others matter little to God. Second, Paul doesn't even judge himself as a success or failure and we shouldn't either. It is often true we can be our own worst critics. To do so is folly. Only God knows in full all that He hopes for us to accomplish. The reality is that we may be doing better than we think! Third, it is important what God thinks of us! Success is being found faithful in doing the jobs we've been given.

And last, God will judge us not only on our performance, but also by the motives of our hearts. This is a great anchor of hope and joy to me. This means that when our best intentions go awry, when our greatest plans fall flat, and when our critics are at our heels, God knows the motives of our hearts and will judge intentions as well as performance. In love He surrounds us in a mighty embrace and says, "It's all right. I know you meant things to turn out differently. Your heart is right and that's the root of faithfulness. Well done, good and faithful servant."

Are you facing a tough assignment? Perhaps, like the church described here, you are dealing with a ministry that seems fruitless and you are tempted to quit and walk away. Perhaps you are thinking about abandoning a difficult marriage, job, or relationship. Let me encourage you to hang in there. Faithfulness may not always bring results we can see and measure, but it is the yardstick by which God measures all believers. What is your faithfulness? It is staying until your job is done, no matter what others think. It is staying until your cry can become one with Christ's, "It is finished!" That's success!

Making It Yours

1. What are some ways people commonly judge success?

2. What standards of comparison did the Pharisees use to distinguish the spiritually successful? (Matt. 3:7-9; 6:1-18)

3. What does Jesus teach us about making financial or material gain the method of measuring success? (Matt. 6:19-24; Luke 12:15-21)

4. Where did John the Baptist say success comes from? (John 3:27)

5. Why wasn't John jealous of Jesus' ministry? (John 3:22-30)

6. What did Jesus mean when He cried, "It is finished!"? (John 17:4-8; 19:28-30)

7. What did Paul mean when he wrote that those who "compare themselves with themselves, they are not wise"? (2 Cor. 10:10-18)

8. Read 1 Corinthians 4:3-5. What four principles for judging success does Paul refer to in this passage?

9. Which of these principles do you most need to apply to your life right now? Why?

This excerpt from From Broken Pieces to a Full Basket: The Positive Side of Failure *by Cheryl M. Smith is reprinted with permission from Christian Publications, 3825 Hartzdale Drive, Camp Hill, PA 17011, copyright 1993.*

chapter seven

What's My *Story?*

Deanna L. Baird & Annette Ford

Sooner or later all of us can get caught in the seemingly harmless comparison trap. Before we realize it, we're being entrapped in a lifestyle that can drain us of all our effectiveness for Christ because we're unhappy with how He made us. According to two women who have been there, there is a better way! Find out more about their personal stories and how they are effectively conquering comparison in their own lives.

"I didn't see it until it was too late. It was as if a full-length mirror had been placed before me and there stood my reflection, a dowdy looking woman in a simple outfit. The comparison continued as dissatisfaction came to life in my mind and heart."

One Sunday I had gone into church, and there in the lobby was the pastor with a couple I did not recognize. A group of my friends had come alongside and were in the process of introducing themselves, but all I could focus on was what this woman was wearing. Now I'm no fashion expert, but this particular outfit was stunning. Living in a rural area such as ours, one rarely comes across someone who dresses so well, and this was a real showstopper.

What I thought was only a look of appreciation had turned into something else. What happened next caught me off guard. The feeling came over me so quickly that I didn't see it until it was too late. It was as if a full-length mirror had been placed before me and there stood my reflection, a dowdy looking woman in a simple outfit. The comparison continued as dissatisfaction came to life in my mind and heart.

The moment I realized what I was doing, I stopped, but not before I saw what "slapping God in the face" looked like. I was sick; it hadn't even been two hours since I had spent time praising God for all that He had blessed me with. In an instant feelings that tore at my heart and revealed a vulnerable area flooded my being.

How should we handle these situations when they come up? Think about the areas in your own life where you are most vulnerable or susceptible. Then pray for the strength to resist the temptation of comparison. Be vigilant. I have found the following practices personally helpful.

First, look for Scriptures that keep your eyes fixed on the Lord, not the things of this world. Colossians 3:2 says, "Set your mind on things above, not on earthly things." We are not to be concerned with the here and now, but the eternal.

Second, we need to keep our lives in perspective, looking at the big picture. You will live more joyfully

> ### LifeLifters
>
> "Joy of life seems to me to arise from a sense of being where one belongs ... All the discontented people I know are trying sedulously to be something they are not, to do something they cannot do. Contentment, and indeed usefulness, comes as the infallible result of great acceptances, great humilities—of not trying to make ourselves this or that to conform to some dramatized version of ourselves—but of surrendering ourselves to the fullness of life—of letting life flow through us."
>
> **—David Grayson—**

with others, and you'll be free to celebrate without the fear of falling into the old trap of envy and bitterness. Trust that God knows how your story unfolds and know He cares for you.

Finally, live "thankfully" all the days of your life. Don't compare your gifts and talents with anyone. First Corinthians 12:1 says, "Now about spiritual gifts, brothers, I do not want you to be ignorant." In other words do not use what you have been given to manipulate others or to serve your own self-interests. We are to use what we are given for a purpose, to further God's kingdom.

Recognizing this problem is not the end of it, or something to take lightly. Living in the consumer age as we do, it will always be easier for us to have more wants than needs. But with a little work and awareness of our own vulnerabilities, we can conquer the comparison trap.

Deanna L. Baird

"I realized that I had believed the lie that I must perform to be worthy, loved, and accepted. Because of this I could not feel God's unconditional love."

I was alone backstage. My performing act was over, my makeup mask washed off, my costume tossed to the side. Lonely and vulnerable, I ached to feel God's love for the real me, not just the masked performer.

The stage was my life as a young church-planter's wife in downtown Toronto. The mask was the smile I painted on my face to cover up my pain and insecurity. The costume was my attempt to look and dress right, to be credible in my role. My act was the flourish of activities I performed, craving acceptance from others, and ultimately from God.

Then one day the curtain closed in my heart. I realized that though the song and dance, bright lights, and applause of people invigorated and flattered me, the performer was not me. It was a well-developed façade. The real me was mask-less, costume-less, alone, afraid to be seen for who I was, and longing to feel truly loved by God. I did not feel worthy unless I proved myself, performed with excellence, and made God proud to be my Father. I knew God's love is unconditional, but I could not feel it. How could God love me, so full of imperfections and insecurities?

Yearning to prove God's unconditional love for

me, I sat down on our living room couch with my Bible and a sheet of paper. Starting in Genesis, I wrote down every reference I could find on God's love for people throughout the Bible. I discovered anew that God's love for me is faithful and everlasting. Knowing me before I was born, He formed me and knit me together to be who I am. I realized that I had believed the lie that I must perform to be worthy, loved, and accepted. Because of this, I could not feel God's unconditional love.

I admitted that the empty glitter of performing and masking myself was worthless, destructive, and alienating. I then declared that because God loves me, He accepts me, changes me, and uses me. He teaches me to understand His love, to accept myself, and to reach out to others. My heart's cry was for God to help me to feel His love, to live unmasked, to obey Him, and not to perform an empty, futile show. I asked Him to help me to live secure, comforted, and unafraid, and to feel accepted and worthwhile in His unfailing love.

God met me in an unforgettable way that day as I prayed this prayer: "I reach out to You, God. My heart is breaking. I need so desperately to feel Your love. I look up with tear-filled eyes and see Your arms lovingly reaching out to hold me. Your tender eyes accept me as me. You have been waiting and waiting for me to come home to Your warm embrace. I am home. I am safe. I am me, in my Father's loving arms."

Annette Ford

chapter eight

Digging Deeper:
Living for
an Audience of One

Kris Grisa

"Man looks at the outward appearance, but the LORD looks at the heart" (1 Sam. 16:7).

While you have heard the truth that performing to please others will short-circuit a right relationship with God, do you still fall into the comparison trap?

What is at the heart of giving others the job of judge over the merits of our performance in life? While we sense that we would be freed from a suffocating burden of stress if we would simply live to please our "Audience of One," we often still willingly fall into the comparison trap. Our critical audience of many has the power to undo us—or exalt us.

Why do we give others (inside and outside of our church community) this power? Perhaps it is as simple as this: we lack the will to wait for our proper reward from our heavenly Father. We mistake the temporal—

the praise of men—for being better than an over-flowing cup of the eternal—the praise of our Father who is in heaven.

We can take steps to correct our attitude. Work your way through the following verses and questions.

Read the following verses from the Sermon on the

LifeLifters

"Don't be a cloud just because you can't be a star."

—**Croft M. Pentz**—

Mount and find the common theme in Jesus' teaching on performance. Meditate on the application of "secrecy" in your own life.

Read: Matthew 6:1, 3, 5, 6, 8, 16, 17, and 32.

Although Jesus lived His life openly for the world's review, read the following passages to remind yourself who His actual audience was as He lived on earth. As you read, ask yourself if Jesus' motivation was always understood. Have you faced the temptation recently to act as people expected you to, even though you knew God called you to do something different?

Read: Luke 2:46-49; John 4:31-34; John 11:41; and John 8:25-30.

If you were to begin to live without regard for "the praise of men," might you find yourself becoming insensitive to the needs and cares of others?

Jesus had simple words to say about the depth of sensitivity that will characterize the actions of one who is solely devoted to the will of His Father. "They will know you are My disciples by your love for one another."

Is there any suggestion in the following passage that the world must be able to judge the disciples' actions as loving? What would happen if our goal was to be certain we were always viewed by others as loving?

Read: John 15:9-17;
then be sure to read on to verses 18-19.

chapter nine

Vitamins
for Volunteers

12 ways to energize the people who help you.

Greg Asimakoupoulos

Although I am still learning how to work with volunteers, here are twelve discoveries I've made that keep helpers happy and healthy. I call them vitamin B-12 boosters.

1. Volunteers give their time—give their best—when they feel appreciated.

Even more than paid staff, volunteers have a need for recognition. Other than the satisfaction of work well done, recognition is their reward. When we supplemented our church office with eight receptionists who donated four hours once a week, we provided each of them with a nameplate. Each week when they come to work, they slide their name into the holder on the reception desk. We can't pay them, but we can certainly assist their feeling of importance and ownership in a ministry that takes individuals seriously. Public praise from the pulpit, hand-engraved certificates, newsletter recognition, and customized thank-you cards—these are just some of the ways ministry assistants in our church are "compensated."

2. Volunteers will do whatever it takes to get the job done when there is flexibility.

For years we struggled with finding people who would make a commitment to teach Sunday school for twelve months. When we finally opted for a rotating schedule (one month on/one month off), we had more than enough to draw from. Our system may not resemble what the textbook on recruitment teaches, but it appears to be more sensitive to the hectic lifestyles our members embrace. When we work to accommodate them at the level of their availability, they are more willing to accommodate us.

3. Volunteers require a detailed job description.

Trust and deadlines may motivate them, but sufficient guidelines are a must if they're going to hit the ground running. Uncertainty breeds anxiety and dissipated energy. Volunteers must be able to restate what it is they think you want them to do. Thoughts unattached to paper are too slippery for comfort. Job descriptions drawn up on paper aren't just for those who draw a salary; volunteers need them too.

4. Volunteers tend to renew their commitments when they are given the authority to do their job.

Contented workers are those who know you will not step in and take control once the assignment has been given. It doesn't matter if you can do a better job. That is not the issue. Letting someone else do "his or her best" so you can find needed rest definitely is.

5. Volunteers need more time than you do to complete a task.

Volunteers struggle with time management as

much as paid professionals. In our church it takes an office helper as much as half an hour to settle in and focus on the job at hand before answering the phone or typing a letter. Like us, unpaid employees are exposed to Procrastinators' Disease (work always expands to fill the time allotted for it) and Murphy's fever (if anything can go wrong in completing a task, it most likely will). When we are more generous with deadlines, not as much will get done, but workers have a lot more enjoyable time getting there. I like what Ted Engstrom repeatedly told his employees at World Vision, "Never do today what can be left until tomorrow." That's the kind of realistic clock that ticks for those who don't punch one.

6. Volunteers perform most productively when they are treated like paid staff.

If not included in regular pastoral staff meetings, those who assist around the church during the week should have a staff meeting of their own facilitated by a lead volunteer. The pastor could be invited to drop in to hear their concerns, brief them on issues of significance affecting the congregation, review his personal calendar, and seek their input. Just yesterday I asked the head of our volunteer receptionists for her insights on how I might respond better to a 'troubled' member of our church she knows quite well. Not only did she give me good advice, but she left her work station feeling like she had contributed to the overall ministry beyond just answering the phones. Paid staff not only have regular staff meetings, they also have Christmas parties, game nights, and dinners at the pastor's home. Why shouldn't the volunteers expect the same?

7. *Volunteers deserve training.*

It's not sufficient to hand them a job description. The receptionist, usher, home Bible study facilitator, worship leader, or Sunday school teacher deserves to know techniques and tips to do the job the pastoral staff envisions. Dr. Robert Boyd Munger gave me a valuable model for training others while I was a student at Fuller Seminary. He said, *"First I do it and you watch me. Then, we do it together. Then, you do it and I'll watch you. And finally, you do it by yourself."*

8. *Volunteers need relational support.*

They need to feel connected. I am always available to my staff, both paid and unpaid. My door may be closed signifying a desire to have my privacy protected, but they know that applies to everybody else *except* them. At times an office assistant may need to pray over an unexpected situation that precludes her from doing her work. Other times the supply clerk may need to talk through a difficulty with a grown son that has him torn up inside. Or it may just be a welcome knock announcing that one of the Bible study leaders has homemade muffins to energize my sermon preparation.

9. *Volunteers need to know there is a freedom to fail.*

Our church chairman was an officer in the military for over twenty-five years. He survived in combat by learning from his mistakes and not being lessened by them. He serves on the church council, leads a home Bible study, and teaches Sunday school. In all of his commitments he has tried a lot of novel programs. Not all of them have succeeded. Nonetheless, he has a reputation in our church for being a successful leader.

Two of his favorite sayings illustrate his approach to life. One he terms the eleventh commandment: "Thou shalt not sweat it!" The other he places with the Beatitudes: "Blessed are those who have permission to change their mind!" If that kind of freedom to fail results in the productivity and servanthood associated with a navy captain, it is worthy of replication.

10. Volunteers need time off.

It doesn't matter if they are payroll or cinnamon-roll rewarded workers. Church work is people work and people work leaves people pooped. Sunday school teachers who are encouraged to take the summer off from teaching (because they teach nine months straight for ten years in a row) are more inclined to return in the fall refreshed with their emotional elastic replenished. The same goes for volunteer custodial help, gardeners, greeters, or worship leaders. A breather is the best investment we can make to guarantee a high-yield return.

11. Volunteers should not be taken for granted.

We come to expect a level of performance and focus primarily on their output. But behind the performance of a highly gifted individual is an individual with hurts and hopes and family issues just like we have. It may delay the project awaiting me on my desk, but the few minutes it takes to stop and inquire about their weekend activity, their spouse's job or their recent prayer request will make a difference. It will remind them that they are donating their time to the greatest institution this side of heaven. It will remind us that they are people first, volunteers second.

12. Volunteers need celebrations.

At our church, we look for reasons to have a party and seize the moment to recognize accomplishment. It's not a novel idea. They do it in the hair salon where I get my hair cut. Every season of the year is recognized by the contests, displays, and wall hangings. They even wear costumes at times. The team of hair stylists obviously enjoys working together. It's because they take time to have fun and celebrate life. What a great example! Those who find reasons to celebrate will laugh more, complain less, and trust each other to a greater degree. We just need to keep our ears open for noteworthy achievements and "seize the day." And guess who sets the atmosphere where celebrations are encouraged? That's right! (Now whose birthday did you forget this week?)

chapter ten

Counseling Corner:
Real Women,
Real Beauty

Ingrid Lawrenz, MSW

*H*ave you ever noticed how most women's magazines have the same features: crash diets and exercises to take inches off your waist, while at the same time showing you photos of high-caloric food? The average American woman is size 14. Yet fashion magazines and advertisers want us to believe average is abnormal, it's wrong. The beauty industry makes over 60 billion dollars a year by inspiring us to feel embarrassed about our bodies. However, their success contributes to 75 percent of American women feeling dissatisfied with their appearance, 5 million having serious eating disorders and 1,000 dying annually from anorexia.

Obsession with image has also infiltrated the church. Some Christian women are holding back from using their gifts due to a self-consciousness about their bodies, and self-disgust is silencing their voices. By shutting down and pulling back, they lose, the church loses, and God loses.

I am a forty-something, athletic, average-sized woman. It's not always easy to feel content with myself, especially when today's model is a flawless size two, but I'm learning. Looking at old pictures of my female relatives—aunts, great aunts, and grandmothers—I see my destiny. They were slender brides, some even looked gaunt during the depression years with frail children hanging on them. Full chests and wide torsos typified their middle age, and a sagging thinness typified their later years. We Americans fight this natural pattern of changing beauty and wisdom that comes with the years. Without Weight Watchers, diet plans, or exercise clubs, those women did their work and raised their families. They were beautiful, godly women, each in her own natural, robust way. It's futile for me to think that time, surgery, or money can alter my genetic code in any significant way, when in reality, only one in 100,000 can conform to the Barbie doll image.

> ### LifeLifters
>
> *"Enjoy your own life without comparing it with that of another."*
>
> **—Marquis de Condorcet—**

God made us like the flowers of the field in all their beauty and glory, each one unique in color, shape and design. Jesus said in Matthew 6:28-30, "See how the lilies of the field grow. They do not labor or spin. Yet I tell you that not even Solomon in all his splendor was dressed like one of these. If that is how God clothes the grass of the field, which is here today and tomorrow is thrown into the fire, will he not much more cloth you?" Our bodies are the uniforms in which we enter and exit this world. Each one is beautiful, each one is different.

Think about the women you've considered beautiful—the ones who have touched your heart and soul. Are they beautiful to you because they could be supermodels or because their character shines through in real beauty? Like it or not, you are a model to your daughters and your sisters in Christ. Half of all nine-year-old girls diet; 90 percent of high school girls do so regularly. Excess attempts at beauty on your part can threaten other women. A real woman of internal beauty becomes a draw, a mentor, and a comfort to those around her. She exudes beauty. When God created the first real woman, Eve, (who knows what size she wore!) He said she was very good.

Many Christian women don't accept their created bodies, and are instead always comparing themselves to a false ideal. They see the marks they've received on their bodies from years of giving out love as defects. Instead, they need to see themselves as seasoned beauties. All of us need to see ourselves and others with Christ's eyes. We have let the world transform our minds instead of Christ. This is an issue believers should seek to change, first in their heads and then in their churches.

Here is a sample prayer you can pray if you're caught in this beauty trap ...

Dear Lord Jesus,

Thank You for making me, forming me, and transforming me into Your image.

Lord, please forgive my vain aspirations and my self-hatred towards my body. I confess to You that I have spent countless hours obsessing over my weight and body shape, ever comparing myself to others. Forgive me for avoiding, withdrawing, and hiding because of a lack of confidence in my appearance and for not using my time to actively love others and use my gifts. Please deliver me from the temptation to fixate on food, weight, and dieting.

Please help me to see my body the way You do. Teach me to treat it with care and to respect it as the temple where Your Holy Spirit dwells. Help me to exercise it, clean it, and feed it properly so it may be healthy and have energy to be useful to You. Thank You for fearfully and wondrously forming me in my mother's womb. Help me to accept and be grateful for the unique genetic shape you encoded into all my cells. Please forgive me for the sin of comparison and competition with other women's looks. Teach me contentment and self-acceptance so that I can forget about myself and my appearance and instead run the race You have set before me, using my body as a vehicle or an instrument of Your bidding.

Thank You for the words of the Song of Solomon (chapter 7) that speak of my beauty as the heap of wheat of my belly and the curves of my thighs. Thank You for my rounded belly that cradled and protected my babies that grew inside me, that cushioned my children's faces as they ran to me for comfort, that soothed them with a soft and tender seat as they snuggled in my lap. Thank You for the fat and estrogen you store there for me in case of emergency.

Lord, thank You for loving me—every wrinkle, roll, and curve. And may the love and beauty of Your character shine through every move, hug, word, smile, and work of my body.

In Jesus' name I pray.

Amen.

chapter eleven

The Place of *No Regrets*

Jackie Katz

Yes, I admit it: I have regrets. I wish I didn't, but I do. I regret that I disciplined my children in anger. I regret that I used anger to control. I regret my impatience and sharp words. I regret my unkind spirit and failure to encourage. I regret it all. Even now that my children are grown, my regrets sometimes accrue such power they erase all memory of the good I did as a mother. Regret has been a familiar and frequent companion.

Regrets are not easy to bear. They breed the "if onlys." If only I could erase the past. If only I could do it over. If only … But we can never turn back the clock. The choices we make today have consequences in the future and we must live with them. It's that old sowing and reaping principle that Scripture talks about. We reap what we sow. Oh, it's not that I haven't asked for forgiveness; I have … many times. I confessed my failures and asked for forgiveness and the children were quick to forgive, but I still regret I did not exercise more self-control.

How can we minimize the "regrets" and the "if onlys?" We need to assess our actions today and do something about them.

In Ephesians 6:4 Paul says, "Fathers, do not provoke your children to anger …" (NASB). Paul here is speaking about a parental issue, one that involves both parents. The word *provoke* here means *to make one beside himself in anger.* This kind of anger is identified by sudden heated outbursts. Parents are to rear their children in such a way that they will not become angry young men and women.

In Colossians 3:21, a similar command is given, "Fathers, provoke not your children to anger, lest they be discouraged" (KJV). The word *provoke* here means to *embitter, stir up, excite, exasperate.* It connotes a turning in of anger as shown by the phrase *lest they be discouraged.* Parents need to discipline their children in such a way that will not "break their children's spirits" or "take the wind out of their sails."

God has placed us in authority over our children, but He warns us not to abuse that power. We are responsible to God for the exercise of that authority, and misusing it carries devastating results, leading not only to regrets.

I invite you to stop and take the simple evaluation below. It will help you identify the ways in which you may be provoking your child to anger, without even realizing it.

Recognizing the Symptoms

1. Outward anger
This child is openly rebellious and explodes in anger against authority. His anger is turned "outward."

He is uncooperative, disrespectful, and has trouble controlling his temper.

2. A wounded and closed spirit

This child's spirit appears broken and closed. He is withdrawn and moody, unresponsive and apathetic, discouraged, or even resistant to authority. His anger is turned "inward" which can lead to bitterness. You can detect a wounded spirit if your child frequently does not entrust you with his deepest secrets.

3. A poor self-image

A large part of your child's self-concept comes from the way he thinks you see him. If he does not "feel" love and respect from you, he concludes that he is a disappointment to you.

A Plan for Action

By now you may want to throw up your hands, turn in your parent badge, and quit. If you feel that you have made a great many mistakes in rearing your children, welcome to the human race! Parenting is not a simple task, and we are not perfect. God in His grace has provided a way to repair relationships.

What can you do if you have been provoking your child to anger?

1. Identify the specific ways you have been provoking your child to anger.

2. Confess these sins to God and ask for His forgiveness. Be sure to accept God's forgiveness for past mistakes. (1 John 1:9).

3. Ask your child to forgive you for the specific things you have done.

Nothing initiates change as much as saying, "I was wrong, will you please forgive me?" (Prov. 28:13).

4. Ask your child if there are other ways in which you have provoked him or her to anger. If he or she reveals other ways, ask for forgiveness. Together, make plans to replace old behaviors with new behaviors (Heb. 10:24).

Trying to raise a child with no regrets is not an easy task. But we can minimize the regrets and the "if onlys" if we assess our actions today and do something about them. So after you take this simple self-evaluation, do your best to follow the plan for action and allow God to bring you to the place of no regrets with your children.

Do I Provoke My Children to Anger?
A Self Evaluation

YES NO

___ ___ Do I lose patience as I wait for my child to finish a task?

___ ___ Do I embarrass and demean my child by comparing him and talking about his shortcomings to others?

___ ___ Do I call my child names like clumsy, stupid, dumb, slow, or sloppy?

___ ___ Do I forget to compliment my child on his good qualities?

___ ___ Have I accepted my child and thanked God for all that he is? (personality, looks, health)

___ ___ Do I lie to my child?

___ ___ Do I tease my child even though I know he does not enjoy it?

YES NO

___ ___ Do I show partiality to one child over another?

___ ___ Do I press my child into activities or hobbies that I prefer instead of allowing him to choose?

___ ___ Do I communicate negative things to my child through nonverbal communication?

___ ___ Do I continually threaten my child but never follow through with appropriate discipline?

___ ___ Do I make promises to my child and then break them?

___ ___ Do I forget to forgive my child?

___ ___ Do I neglect to admit when I am wrong and ask for forgiveness?

___ ___ Do I listen when my child is talking to me?

___ ___ Do I abuse my child physically by punching, kicking, slapping, shaking, throwing, beating, or shoving?

___ ___ Am I constantly finding fault with my child, with statements such as, "How come you missed … You didn't … You forgot …?"

___ ___ Do I demand too much of my child intellectually, spiritually, physically, or emotionally?

___ ___ Do I overprotect my child by never allowing any liberty and not trusting him?

___ ___ Do I criticize my child in front of others?

Author Biographies

Jill Briscoe is a popular writer and conference speaker who has authored over forty books. She directs Telling the Truth media ministries with her husband, Stuart, and ministers through speaking engagements around the world. Jill is executive editor of *Just Between Us*, a magazine for ministry wives and women in leadership, and serves on the boards of World Relief and Christianity Today International. Jill and Stuart live in suburban Milwaukee, Wisconsin, and have three grown children and thirteen grandchildren.

Meredith R. Sheppard is the author of "Wives in Touch," a newsletter offering encouragement, hope and practical advice to pastors' wives throughout the United States. She has also written for several Christian publications and has an active speaking ministry. Meredith serves alongside her husband, Paul, at Abundant Life Christian Fellowship in Menlo Park, California. They have two teenagers.

Michele Halseide is a freelance writer for numerous Christian organizations, businesses and publications. Michele has also served as contributing editor for *Today's Christian Woman* magazine. Working for a national Christian radio program, she was actively involved in writing copy and interviewing hosts on the air for three years. Today, as a founder of Reaching Higher, a Christian School for Accelerated Learning, Michele teaches writing. Michele also runs a Christian bookstore and coffeehouse. She lives in Sheridan, Wyoming, with her husband, Phil, and three children.

Anita Haney has been a pastor's wife for twenty-eight years. Anita is the author of *Battling Anorexia—A Deadly Trap.* After five-and-a-half years of ministry in Lebanon, Missouri, Anita and her husband are taking a short sabbatical, living in Cookeville, Tennessee. They have three grown children.

Shelly Esser has been the editor of Just Between Us, a magazine for ministry wives and women in leadership, for the last thirteen years. She has written numerous published articles and ministered to women for over twemtu years. Her recent book, *My Cup Overflows—A Deeper Study of Psalm 23* encourages women to discover God's shepherd love and care for them. She lives in Germantown, Wisconsin, with her husband, John, and four daughters.

Cheryl M. Smith is the author of two books, *From Broken Pieces to a Full Basket: The Positive Side of Failure* and *Kindling A Kindred Spirit: A Woman's Guide to Intimate Christian Fellowship.* Cheryl is also a seasoned speaker. She and her husband, Scott, live in Sylvania, Ohio, where they minister at Westgate Chapel. They have two teenagers.

Deanna L. Baird is a freelance writer who makes her home in Armada, Michigan with her husband, David, and their two children. She enjoys writing and is currently working as a library aide, where she has the opportunity to help others develop a love for reading.

Annette Ford has lived in five countries while growing up as a missionary kid. Annette works alongside her husband, Stephen, as a missionary in Hungary. They have two children.

Kris Grisa has spent many years involved in small group leadership. She is an avid disciple maker, teaching women and girls in small group settings through her local church. Kris is also a writer of devotional materials. She and her husband, John, live in Brookfield, Wisconsin, with their three children.

Greg Asimakoupoulos is an ordained minister and freelance writer. His articles have appeared regularly in a variety of Christian periodicals. Greg has also authored several books including, *The Time Crunch, Jesus, the People's Choice, Prayers from My Pencil and Heroic Faith*. Greg and his wife, Wendy, have three daughters and live in Naperville, Illinois.

Ingrid Lawrenz, MSW is a licensed social worker who has been counseling for seventeen years. Ingrid has been a pastor's wife for twenty-seven years and is currently the senior pastor's wife at Elmbrook Church in suburban Brookfield, Wisconsin. She and her husband, Mel, have two teenagers and live in Waukesha, Wisconsin.

Jackie Katz received her ministry training at Philadelphia Biblical University. She is an experienced teacher and communicator, biblical counselor, and has been a columnist for *Just Between Us*, a magazine for ministry wives and women in leadership. She brings a mix of insight, humor and practicality that encourages God's gift of hope and joy in all she does. She and her husband have partnered in ministry for thirty-nine years. They have two grown children and seven grandchildren and live in Spring Grove, Pennsylvania.

Dealing with Difficult People

Handling problem
people in your life.
ISBN 0-78143-951-5
ITEM #102350

Finding God's Will

Embracing God's plan
for your life.
ISBN 0-78143-947-7
ITEM #102346

Finding Joy

Developing patterns
for a joyful life.
ISBN 0-78143-949-3
ITEM #102348

Keeping Fresh
When You're Frantic

Renewing your spiritual life.
ISBN 0-78143-956-6
ITEM #102355

**To get these excellent resources, visit us online at
www.cookministries.com or call 1-800-323-7543!**

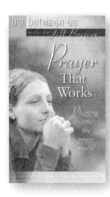

Prayer that Works
Plugging into the
power source.
ISBN 0-78143-953-1
ITEM #102352

Resolving Conflict
Stilling the storms of life.
ISBN 0-78143-954-X
ITEM #102353

The Search for Balance
Keeping first things first.
ISBN 0-78143-955-8
ITEM #102354

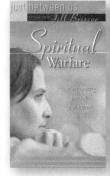

Spiritual Warfare
Equipping yourself for battle.
ISBN 0-78143-948-5
ITEM #102347